PUFFIN BOOKS

AMMA, TAKE ME TO TIRUPATI

Bhakti Mathur took to writing in 2010 when she created the popular Amma, Tell Me series of children's picture books about Indian festivals and mythology. After a long stint as a banker, she now juggles her time between her writing, her passion for fitness and long-distance running, and her family. She lives in Hong Kong with her husband, their two children and two dogs. When not writing or running after her young boys, Bhakti is happiest curled up with a book in one hand and a hot cup of chai in the other. To know more, visit her at www.bhaktimathur.com.

Priyankar Gupta is an animation film designer and visual storyteller. He is associated with various publishing houses as an illustrator for children's books and also works as a pre-visualizer for TV commercials and feature films. He is a visiting faculty member and mentor in various design institutes across the country.

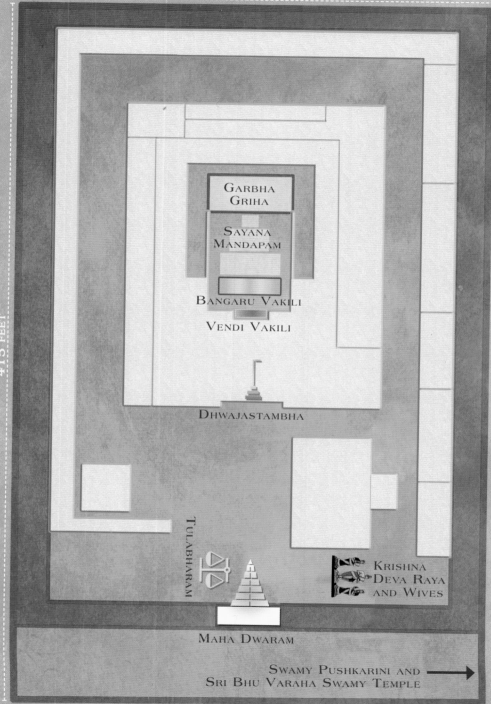

263 FEET

415 FEET

GARBHA
GRIHA

SAYANA
MANDAPAM

BANGARU VAKILI

VENDI VAKILI

DHWAJASTAMBHA

TULABHARAM

KRISHNA
DEVA RAYA
AND WIVES

MAHA DWARAM

SWAMY PUSHKARINI AND
SRI BHU VARAHA SWAMY TEMPLE

AREA OF THE MAIN TEMPLE: 2.2 ACRES

Amma, Take Me to Tirupati

BHAKTI MATHUR

Illustrations by Priyankar Gupta

PUFFIN BOOKS

An imprint of Penguin Random House

For Anurag, who brings me sunshine

PUFFIN BOOKS

USA | Canada | UK | Ireland | Australia
New Zealand | India | South Africa | China

Puffin Books is part of the Penguin Random House group of companies
whose addresses can be found at global.penguinrandomhouse.com

Published by Penguin Random House India Pvt. Ltd
7th Floor, Infinity Tower C, DLF Cyber City,
Gurgaon 122 002, Haryana, India

First published in Puffin Books by Penguin Random House India 2017

Text copyright © Bhakti Mathur 2017
Series copyright © Penguin Random House India 2017
Illustrations copyright © Priyankar Gupta 2017

All rights reserved

10 9 8 7 6 5 4 3 2 1

ISBN 9780143428312

Typeset in Agmena Pro
Book design and layout by Neelima P Aryan
Printed at Replika Press Pvt. Ltd, India

www.penguin.co.in

CONTENTS

 AUTHOR'S NOTE

The Amma Take Me series is an attempt to introduce children to the major Indian religions and faiths through their important places of worship. Styled as the travelogues of a mother and her two young children, these books link history, tradition and mythology to bring alive the major temples, churches, mosques and mausoleums of India in an engaging and non-preachy way.

The stories emphasize universal values and the message of love and tolerance central to all faiths. I hope that this journey of Amma and her children will inspire you to embark on your own travels with your children, and I hope that you will enjoy reading these books as much as I enjoyed writing them.

Lastly, these works are a reflection of my personal interpretation of the faith and traditions that these timeless monuments represent. I am far from being an authority on religion or on Indian religious history, and while I have made every effort to ensure that the factual and historical information in these books is correct, I do not assume and hereby disclaim any liability to any party for any loss, damage or disruption caused by errors or omissions.

Amma, Shiv and Veer looked up in wonder at the sight in front of them. Not a word passed between them for a few minutes. The rolling hills, covered in a carpet of lush green, towered before them as if to touch the sky. Waterfalls gushed down the red sandstone cliffs in a series of mini cascades, like strands of silver thread suspended against the hillside. The morning sun reflected off the mountain lakes and threw flashes of light that darted and danced across the green valleys.

The three of them were at the foothills of the Tirumala range and were about to start their journey up the most sacred of the seven hills to the site of the famous Sri Venkateswara Swamy Temple, also known as the Tirupati Balaji temple.

'This is not just another temple, boys!' said Amma as the car that they had rented for the day purred up the hill. 'It is one of the most visited places of worship in the world. Tens of thousands of people visit the temple every single day of the year, and on some special days the count goes up to more than a hundred thousand!'

'Wow!' exclaimed Shiv, his mind racing to make sense of the numbers. 'That's like a cricket stadium full of people at the temple every day!'

'But why?' jumped in Veer. 'What's so special about it, Amma?'

'The great god Vishnu himself is believed to have lived on this hill and the temple is dedicated to him,' answered Amma. 'He is known as Venkateswara, which means "the remover of sins", and the hill is named Venkatadri after him. People have been coming here for more than a thousand years and believe that a prayer to Venkateswara does not go unanswered for he has the power to make their wishes come true.'

'Can I pray to Venkateswara and wish for something too?' asked Veer. 'Will he listen to me?'

'Of course you can! But I think he may have already heard your prayers!' Amma said with a big smile as she reached inside her purse to fish out two bars of their favourite chocolate.

The two children grabbed the offering and, unwrapping the bars quickly, took their first blissful bites of the chocolate. Chomping merrily, they looked out of the window, ready to catch their first glimpse of the famous temple. A cool breeze blew across their faces as the car made its way along the winding road up to the peak. Rows of red, pink and yellow bougainvillea bushes lined the broad road, their flower-like spring leaves waving gaily. The route was dotted with signboards that read *Om Venkatesaya Namah*— 'Salutations to Lord Venkateswara'—and the sound of Om wafted from loudspeakers attached to electricity poles, reverberating across the hills. A few caramel-coloured deer grazing on the hillside looked up at them with big, innocent eyes as they passed by, drawing a shout of delight from Shiv.

'Look, Amma!' he said, pointing at the deer. 'I didn't know there were animals in the forest on this hill. Are there others too?'

'I don't know about other animals, but I do know about a giant snake who lives here,' said Amma, smiling mischievously.

'What? A giant snake!' exclaimed Veer, taken aback. 'You're joking, aren't you?' he added when he saw Amma smile.

'Don't worry. He's not dangerous,' assured Amma. 'We have some time before we reach the temple. Are you boys ready for your first story of the day?'

Both of them nodded eagerly. 'We're always ready for a story, Amma!' said Shiv.

'Here we go, then,' began Amma. 'According to an ancient legend, these hills are actually the coiled body of an enormous divine snake called Adishesha or Shesh Naag, who is Vishnu's loyal friend and also his guardian. Once, the powerful wind god, Vayu, went to visit Vishnu at his home on the heavenly Mount Vaikuntha. Adishesha was standing guard at the entrance and he blocked Vayu's way.

'"You may not enter," said Adishesha firmly. "My master is busy right now and cannot be interrupted."

'"How dare you stop me!" roared Vayu, who was a bit of a hothead. "Don't you know who I am?"

'"I don't care who you are," said the snake, baring his fangs. "You will *not* enter till my master is ready to receive you."

'"Is that right? And who's going to stop me? *You?*" Vayu said mockingly.

'Vishnu heard the loud voices at his doorstep and came out to investigate. He found Adishesha and Vayu locking horns, each boasting about how he was more powerful

than the other. Vishnu tried to reason with them, but to no avail. Instead, the two turned to Vishnu and demanded that he decide who was the stronger being.

'"The only way to decide this is a contest," suggested Vishnu. "I have an idea. Adishesha, why don't you climb Mount Meru and hold the mountain in your coils as firmly as you can, while you, Vayu, try to dislodge Adishesha. Whoever succeeds will be the stronger of the two!"

'They both agreed. Upon reaching Mount Meru, Adishesha wound his massive coils round and round the mountain, all the way up, until his hood covered the peak. Seeing this, Vayu started blowing as hard as he could. He sent tornadoes, whirlwinds and hurricanes to blow the snake off the mountain, but Adishesha held on tightly. Several days and nights of furious combat passed by but neither contestant yielded even though they had both begun to tire. Then suddenly, the winds died down and silence enveloped the mountain. Adishesha thought that Vayu had given up and he lowered his guard, raising his head from the mountaintop to look up for a second. In that moment, Vayu summoned all of his divine might and blew as hard as he could. Adishesha and part of the hill were whisked away and they landed on earth, at this very spot. Adishesha was so dejected by his defeat that he continued to lie where he had fallen and refused to return to the heavens.

'To appease him, Vishnu said, "My dear friend, don't be disheartened. We will be together on earth as we were in heaven. I will come and live with you here, and you will take the form of a magnificent mountain range that people will visit and worship for the ages to come."

'So that is the legend of how these hills came to be,' said Amma. 'The seven peaks that you see are said to be the seven hoods of the great snake Adishesha!'

'So we are actually driving up Adishesha's back!' said Shiv, gazing at the hills to see if he could make out the coils of the snake.

'Did Vishnu keep his promise to come to earth and live with Adishesha?' asked Veer, not wanting the story to end.

'Of course,' replied Amma. 'He lived on this hill and it's even named after him—remember? There are so many stories and legends about Vishnu and these hills that it would take me hours to tell you all of them.'

'Amma, tell us just one!' said Veer, looking at her pleadingly.

'Okay, only one before we reach the top!' said Amma, relenting. 'This story is from the time when Vishnu took the form of a man—Venkateswara—and came to earth in search of his wife, Goddess Lakshmi. She had left him after an argument between them. He travelled far and wide in his quest, but I guess it's not easy to find an angry goddess who doesn't want to be found! Eventually, he arrived in these hills, tired and crestfallen, and sat down to meditate under a tamarind tree. So deep was his meditation that he did not stir for weeks, so much so that a colony of ants formed an anthill around him.

'Worried about his well-being, the gods Brahma and Shiva took the form of a cow and a calf and became part of the herd belonging to the king who ruled over the lands here. The king's cattle would graze in these hills every day, and the divine cow would sneak off to where Vishnu was meditating. She would stand on the anthill and empty her udder over it, pouring out all her milk, thus getting Vishnu—who was submerged under the anthill—some nourishment.

'Puzzled as to why the new cow did not produce any milk when he tried milking her, the cowherd followed her and the calf one day and saw her spraying her milk on the anthill. In a fit of rage, he hurled his axe at the cow. Vishnu sensed the danger to the cow

and jumped out of the anthill to come in the way of the axe. The blade passed perilously close to him, its sharp edge shaving off some of his hair and, along with it, a part of his scalp. Shocked to see a man appear from the anthill, the cowherd fainted.'

'Then what happened?' asked Veer, wide-eyed.

'Just then, a princess called Neela Devi—a divine being—who happened to be passing through the forest, came upon the scene,' said Amma. 'She was struck by the beauty of the young man. *Such a handsome face—and without hair? This cannot be!* she mused. Without thinking of her own looks, she cut off some of her beautiful long hair and, using

9

her magical powers, implanted it on Venkateswara's head. Knowing how precious her lustrous tresses must have been to her, Vishnu was deeply moved by this sacrifice. He thanked her and pronounced, "From this day on, any hair gifted to me by my devotees will belong to you, Neela Devi. I will bless all who donate their hair to me, for in doing so they will be helping me repay your kindness."

'One of these seven hills is named Neeladri after Neela Devi,' finished Amma. 'And that, Veer, is the last story you get before we reach the top.'

Veer flashed a smile of thanks at Amma and turned to join Shiv in taking in the scenery. As their car turned around the next curve, they saw a long, covered walkway snaking up the steep slopes of the hill and, on it, an endless stream of people climbing to the top.

'Amma, are all these people walking up to the temple?' asked Shiv.

'Yes, they are!' replied Amma. 'And it will take them hours to get there. People do it to show how much they love Venkateswara. In fact, some of them climb up on their hands and knees.'

'Ouch!' exclaimed Shiv. 'That must hurt.'

'I want to walk up as well,' said Veer, adding quickly, 'but not on my knees!'

'Maybe next time, when we have more time and you're a bit older,' said Amma, rumpling his hair. 'Did you know it takes four hours to walk up the nearly 4000 steps to reach the hilltop?'

'Wow!' breathed Veer.

'Veer, look!' shouted Shiv, pointing to the peak that had just come in sight as their car turned along yet another curve.

Brilliantly lit up by the morning sun and nestled against the green backdrop of the thickly forested hill stood a tall pyramid-shaped ivory-coloured tower or gopuram. There it was: One of the most popular temples in the world—Sri Venkateswara Swamy Temple of Tirupati. Amma, Shiv and Veer were captivated by the first sight of the famous shrine.

Their car soon reached the top of the hill and they drove through an elaborate arched gateway supported by white and gold pillars, which welcomed visitors to the temple town of Tirumala. On either side of the gateway stood a giant stone statue of a warrior.

'Who are they, Amma?' asked Shiv, pointing at the impressive figures.

'Their names are Jaya and Vijaya, and they are the gatekeepers of Vaikuntha, Vishnu's heavenly abode,' said Amma. 'They are here to greet us in Vishnu's home on earth!'

They arrived at the car park near the main temple and after thanking their driver, Amma, Shiv and Veer got off the car to explore the town on foot. Walking past a crowded row of shops selling everything from statues of Hindu gods, flowers and temple offerings to souvenirs, snacks and a jumble of knick-knacks and trinkets, they came upon a vast open quadrangle in front of the main temple complex. The gopuram, which they had first seen from the road while coming up the hill, towered over them. Before the high temple wall was a tall rectangular stone doorway that marked the entrance. The impressive ivory temple tower was even more magnificent from closer up. The gently tapering walls of the fifty-foot-high, five-storeyed tower were adorned with intricately carved stone statues of Hindu gods and goddesses; and its apex was capped with seven golden inverted pots called *kalasam*s. The rolling green slopes of the Tirumala hills rising up in the background made for the perfect setting for the majestic structure.

'Can we go inside, Amma?' asked Shiv. 'I want to see Venkateswara.'

'Yes, we can, but not now,' replied Amma.

'Why can't we go now?' said Veer impatiently.

'Because I've arranged for us to visit the temple later,' said Amma firmly and walked ahead across the courtyard.

Veer and Shiv grumbled for a few minutes as they tagged along behind her but, taken up by the sights and sounds of their colourful surroundings, they soon forgot what they were upset about. The courtyard was teeming with devotees. People simply stood around or walked about the square, taking in the sacred view that they had travelled from far and wide to see. Some visitors were taking family photos, carefully framing them to ensure the famous gopuram was perfectly placed in the background. Women wearing bright

silk saris and fine gold jewellery stood out from the men, who were mostly dressed in plain half-sleeved shirts and starched white dhotis. Children ran around their parents, happily biting into the biggest laddus that Shiv and Veer had ever seen. But many of the men, women and children they saw had one thing in common—their shaven heads.

'Why are there so many bald people here, Amma?' asked Veer in surprise.

'And why are their heads painted yellow?' questioned Shiv.

Amma smiled. 'Have you already forgotten the story of Neela Devi?' she asked.

Veer thought for a second and then his face lit up. 'I get it,' he said proudly. 'People are giving their hair to help Venkateswara keep his promise to Neela Devi!'

'That's right, they are,' said Amma. 'This temple is also famous for the large number of people who get their heads shaved here. Did you know that there are more than 600 barbers who work for the temple and that they cut the hair of thousands and thousands of devotees every day?'

'I can't believe it!' said Shiv, amazed, looking up at all the shaven heads in the crowd around them.

'I read somewhere that the barbers here cut almost a ton of hair every day,' continued Amma.

'Oh, I know how much that is. That's how much a rhinoceros weighs!' said Veer with a smug smile. 'But where are the barbers, Amma?' he asked, scanning the courtyard.

'Very clever, Veer! I didn't know that fact about rhinos,' Amma said. 'Well, the barbers work in a building nearby called Kalyana Katta, which means "a place where good deeds are done" in Telugu. The yellow paint you see on people's heads is cooling sandalwood paste that the barbers apply on the newly shaven scalps to protect them from the hot sun here.'

'What happens to all the hair?' asked Shiv. 'Do they throw it away?'

'No, they put it to good use,' Amma replied. 'They sell it to companies who make wigs and the money raised from this is used for running the temple and the many charities that it supports.

'Now, unless you want a haircut, we'd better move along. We have an early start tomorrow and I want to show you two special sites before we head back to the car.' Amma ushered the boys across the courtyard.

A short distance ahead, they came upon a large rectangular stone tank with steps on all four sides that led down to a pool of water. A covered pavilion with a golden dome adorned with beautiful carvings and supported by stone pillars

stood in the middle of the pool. People were taking dips in the water with their hands folded in front of them while others sat on the steps, enjoying the peacefulness of their surroundings.

'This is Swamy Pushkarini or "the lake of lotus flowers",' explained Amma. 'It is believed that this lake was brought here from the heavens for Vishnu when he lived on earth and that he used to bathe here every day.'

'Vishnu's own swimming pool!' exclaimed Veer.

'Yes, you can say that,' said Amma, laughing. 'These are sacred waters and a bath in this pool is said to purify one's body and mind. Many devotees take a cleansing dip before they enter the main temple.'

'Can we go for a swim?' asked Shiv. 'I swear we won't be long.'

'But we're not carrying a change of clothes for you,' said Amma. 'You can have a dip tomorrow, I promise.'

She shepherded the two children away from the pool and walked forward to a small stone temple capped with a single white dome. The temple was decorated with garlands of orange and red marigold flowers, and above the entrance was a statue of a goddess in a red sari, flanked by two white elephants.

'Who is that?' asked Veer.

'That is a statue of Goddess Lakshmi welcoming devotees to the temple of Sri Bhu Varaha Swamy. It is tradition to pay him a visit before calling on Sri Venkateswara,' said Amma as they joined the queue of people waiting to enter the temple.

'Who is Varaha Swamy, Amma?' asked Veer curiously. 'And why do we have to see him first?'

'He is another form of Vishnu, in which he appeared to save the world from evil,' answered Amma. 'According to an ancient Hindu tale, the world was once under attack from a wicked demon named Hiranyaksha. Armed with a boon from the god Brahma that made him all-powerful, the demon started terrorizing beings on earth. Then he did something unimaginable. In his arrogance, he decided that all of earth belonged to him and so he dragged the entire planet to the very bottom of the ocean. Mother Earth cried for help as she was submerged in the waters and all life faced extinction.'

'What happened then?' asked Shiv, wide-eyed and totally engrossed in the story.

'The gods panicked and rushed to the great Vishnu for help. They pleaded with him to save the earth from the clutches of the evil Hiranyaksha. Vishnu agreed. He decided to take the form of a boar, known as *varaha* in Sanskrit, when warned about Brahma's boon that protected the demon against gods, humans and all kinds of creatures. But the demon had luckily forgotten to include the boar in the list of animals to which he was immune.

'Assuming the form of a gigantic white boar, Vishnu descended from the heavens. Letting out a terrifying battle roar, he dived deep into the ocean in search of the demon. Hiranyaksha, who believed he was invincible, rushed towards the creature that had dared to challenge him. Thousands of feet below the surface of the water, a fierce battle took place between the two. Weapons whirled, blows were exchanged and the two opponents looked to be evenly matched, till finally, with a ferocious thrust of his mighty tusks, the boar slew the demon. The victorious Varaha then appeared from the waters with his

feet placed on the divine snake Adishesha and the earth balanced on his giant tusks. Everyone breathed a sigh of relief and life on earth was restored.

'Awed by this omnipotent form of Vishnu, people started to worship Varaha and begged him to stay back on earth as its protector. Sri Varaha agreed and decided to make his home in these very hills,' finished Amma.

'Right here?' asked Veer, pointing to the temple.

'Yes,' answered Amma. 'This region is also known as Adi Varaha Kshetra, which means "the land of Varaha". In fact, much later, when Vishnu took the form of Venkateswara and arrived here in search of Lakshmi, he is said to have met Sri Varaha, who still lived here as the lord of these hills.'

'Venkateswara met Varaha?' repeated Shiv, a bit puzzled. 'But aren't they the same person? How were they both here at the same time?'

'Yes, they are both incarnations of Vishnu, but they are different forms of him,' explained Amma. 'Legend has it that Venkateswara asked Varaha to rent him some land in these hills to live on, but he had no money to pay as rent. So he promised to pay Varaha back by asking his devotees to first offer their prayers to Sri Varaha and seek his blessings and only then visit Venkateswara.'

Just as Amma was finishing the story, they reached the front of the queue. A magnificent statue of Sri Varaha sitting on an intricately carved throne was before them. He had the body of a man and the head of a boar. A white mark of camphor extended from the top of his forehead down to his nose. A priest wearing a white dhoti and kurta stood next to the statue with a large silver plate in his hand. On the plate was an oil lamp with a few cotton wicks burning brightly, together with rose petals and grains of rice. The priest performed the *aarti*, moving the thali in a rhythmic circular motion in front of the statue of Sri Varaha. Then he turned to face Amma, Shiv and Veer, gently throwing a few rose petals and grains of rice on them and extending the plate forward. Amma cupped her hands over the flame of the lamp and raised her palms to her forehead. Shiv and Veer copied her.

'Why do we do that when we visit temples, Amma?' asked Shiv.

'And why did the priest throw flowers on us?' asked Veer.

'The questions never stop with you two! Let's move out of the way so that the people behind can get a chance to see him as well,' said Amma as she led them out of the temple. 'Also, the flowers and the flames of the aarti are a way of getting the blessings of Sri Varaha, so that you can become as strong and intelligent as him!'

Amma looked at her watch as they returned to the temple entrance. 'It's almost six o'clock. I've booked us a room in a hotel here. Let's have dinner first and then go check in,' she said. 'Are you boys ready for some more of the cheese dosas you liked so much? I want you in bed straight after dinner, though. We have a very early start tomorrow!'

Shiv turned to Amma with a frown. 'You've done it again, Amma,' he said accusingly. 'We have to get up in the middle of the night to visit another temple, don't we?'

Amma laughed softly. 'Busted!' she said. 'Yes, we have to wake up very early, but trust me, it will be worth it. We are going to a very special prayer ceremony at the temple, called Suprabhatam, which literally means "good morning". You are lucky that you've got the opportunity, as people wait for months and months for this chance. And after that, you can see Venkateswara. So stop scowling. You can have extra dessert at dinner if you promise to go to bed straight after!'

The prospect of extra dessert stopped further protests from the boys, but they continued to grumble to each other as they trailed behind Amma to the car park.

It was a clear, cloudless night, a few hours before dawn. The full moon was like a giant pearl hanging by an invisible string from the star-studded sky, splashing its silver beams on Amma, Shiv and Veer as they arrived at the shrine.

Earlier, Amma had struggled to get them out of bed.

'Why do we have to wake up in the middle of the night every time to go to a temple?' Shiv had groaned as he'd rubbed his eyes.

'I am *so* sleepy,' Veer had complained, pulling the blanket back over his head.

'C'mon, you two! We don't want to miss out on what we came here to see. So stop your complaining and get out of bed at once,' Amma had scolded the boys.

The boys had whined their way out of bed and all through the short drive to the temple. The temple complex was sleepy and quiet at this hour—a sharp contrast to the noise and the crowds of the previous day. The three of them were ushered into a waiting area within, where about 200 people had gathered.

Shiv and Veer looked around the throng of people waiting with them. There was a young mother humming softly as she rocked a sleeping baby in her arms. They waved at a little girl who was sitting on her father's shoulders, and she smiled at them shyly. A newly married couple, still dressed in what seemed to be their wedding finery, held hands as they whispered to each other. An old woman stood clutching a thin prayer book at which she glanced from time to time. Soon, their short wait was over, as suddenly the congregation moved forward, taking them along. Fervent cries of 'Govinda! Govinda! Govinda!' filled the air.

Shiv tugged at Amma's arm and she bent down to listen. 'Why is everyone saying Govinda?' he asked.

'It's one of the many names of Krishna, who is another avatar of Vishnu,' she replied.

'Govinda! Govinda! Govinda!' repeated Shiv and Veer, fully awake by now, as the excitement of the crowd rubbed off on them. Amma smiled and joined in the chorus too. They walked along a covered passageway that snaked its way around the temple and past several large empty rooms adjacent to the walkway.

'Amma, what are all these rooms for?' asked Shiv.

'These are waiting rooms for people to rest in while they wait for their turn to see Venkateswara,' replied Amma. 'Remember, the temple attracts tens of thousands of visitors every day and they have to stand in line for hours to see the famous idol for just a few seconds.'

'People wait for so long to see him for just a few seconds!' said Shiv. 'But why?'

'Remember, I told you—because they believe their prayers will come true,' Amma said. 'They wish they could see Venkateswara for longer but, with so many people waiting their turn, that's all the time one can get. Still, even a few seconds in front of one's God are precious and worth the long wait.'

The gathering kept moving like a slow, meandering river as they passed through more passageways and twisting staircases. The chants grew louder and louder, reaching a crescendo when the temple doors came into sight. Massive brass doors, sectioned into small metal squares—with a copper statue of a warrior on either side—stood in front of them. The familiar gopuram rose above the doorway.

'This is the main entrance of the temple, called Maha Dwaram, meaning "great door",' said Amma. 'The two statues that you see are of the guardians of Lord Venkateswara's treasures. Their names are Sankanidhi and Padmanidhi.'

'Is there real treasure inside, Amma?' asked Shiv. 'Will we get to see it?'

'Yay! A treasure hunt!' exclaimed Veer.

'Yes, we will see the treasure soon,' said Amma, before adding sternly, 'And no, Veer, this is *not* a treasure hunt.'

The three now found themselves following the throng into a large courtyard.

'Amma, look!' piped up Shiv, pointing to a set of ten-foot-high weighing scales up

ahead. A little girl, about two years old, was happily perched on one of the dishes of the scales while her mother stood behind and a priest placed a few bags on the other scale.

'What are they doing with the baby, Amma?' asked Shiv as they walked up to the instrument to get a closer look.

'They are weighing the baby, of course,' replied Amma. 'These scales are called *tula* and what they are doing is called Tulabharam. In ancient times, the emperor himself used to sit on one dish of these scales and was weighed against gold coins, fruit and grain, which were then distributed among the poor. Nowadays, when people have a baby, they come here to thank Venkateswara and donate an amount of rice and fruit equal to the weight of the child. Isn't that a nice thing to do?'

'Can I stand on the scales? You can weigh me in lollipops and we can give them to all the children here . . . and I can keep a few as well,' said Veer with a sly smile.

'Nice try, Veer,' said Amma, laughing, as they moved on to keep up with the rest of the devotees.

Within a few steps, they came upon a tall copper statue of a man, adorned with beautiful ornaments and dressed in green and red silk, with his hands folded in a namaste.

'Who is this, Amma?' asked Shiv.

'This is a statue of Emperor Venkatapati Raya of the Vijayanagara Empire, who ruled over southern India around 500 years ago,' said Amma. 'He and the emperors before him were devotees of Venkateswara and donated a lot of land and money to the temple. His statue stands here to remind us of his generosity.'

Further ahead was a long pavilion held up by rows of intricately carved pillars on all four sides. A unique smaller four-pillared pavilion stood in the centre and, as they got nearer, they saw that each of the pillars was actually made up of four even smaller pillars and was engraved with elaborate carvings. Shiv and Veer marvelled at the figures of warriors astride lions that were atop elephants and horses, which were standing on their hind legs planted on more lions!

'There's Krishna dancing on the snake's head and . . . there's Vishnu riding the divine eagle Garuda,' said Amma, pointing out the sculptures on the pillars. 'Oh, and there's Rama holding his bow!'

The boys were fascinated by the images hewn out of stone, and Amma had to drag them away.

Next, they came to a massive gilded column standing on a broad rectangular base, which was covered with golden sheets engraved with elaborate images of Krishna, Garuda, Hanuman and other Hindu celestial beings. A few people were prostrating themselves before the pillar while others were touching their foreheads to it.

'Why are they doing that, Amma?' asked Veer.

'They are asking for the gods' blessings,' replied Amma. 'Can you spot any gods that you know?'

'Look, that's Krishna lifting Mount Govardhan!' said Shiv, pointing to a striking scene on the huge pillar.

'And Hanuman carrying the mountain!' said Veer excitedly.

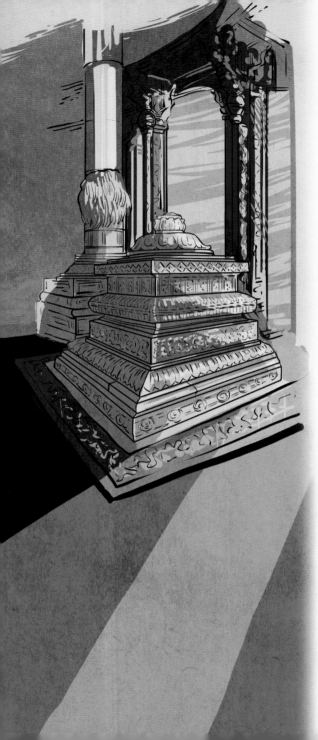

'Correct! The pillar is called Dhwajastambha, which means "flagpole",' said Amma. 'On important festivals, like the Brahmotsavam, a flag with Garuda's symbol is hoisted here. It is an invitation to everyone to come and join the celebrations.'

'What is Brahmotsavam?' asked Veer.

'Brahmotsavam is the biggest festival celebrated in Tirupati, over a period of nine days every October,' said Amma. 'Hundreds of thousands of people take part in the festivities, thronging the streets and every nook and corner of the complex. It is as if the entire world descends on Tirumala. Legend has it that Brahma himself established this celebration to honour Vishnu, the great protector of the universe. Processions with idols of Venkateswara are taken out on the streets with great fanfare. It's as though the god himself comes out of the temple to meet his devotees. The idols are carried on different *vahana*s or vehicles, such as Garuda, Adishesha and Hanuman.'

'But Amma, when are we going to see Venkateswara?' said Shiv.

'Yes, Amma, we simply can't wait any more!' urged Veer.

'Not too long now,' promised Amma as the three passed through a pair of huge silver doors. 'These are called Vendi Vakili, which means "gates of silver".'

Stepping through the shiny doors, they found themselves in another open courtyard. Suddenly, Amma, Shiv and Veer stopped. For glimmering before them was a house of gold, the gateway to the sanctum sanctorum, the Garbha Griha—the home of Venkateswara! And above it rose the famous three-storeyed golden dome, Ananda Nilayam, 'the abode of happiness'. Moonlight poured from the skies on to the dome like the milk of the gods.

Shiv's eyes opened even wider as he stared ahead. Two men, wearing yellow dhotis, with their chests bare, lay prostrate on the cold stone floor, their hands extended in front of them in a namaste. Then they started rolling on the ground, around the sanctum, chanting, 'Govinda! Govinda! Govinda!' with their folded hands still outstretched over their heads.

'What are they doing, Amma?' asked Shiv.

'This ritual is called Angapradakshinam,' said Amma. 'People perform it by rolling on the hard stone floor around the temple.'

'Wow!' said Veer. 'But why are they doing this? Doesn't it hurt?'

'I'm sure it does,' said Amma, 'and yet there is a long list of devotees who wait for months before they get their turn to do Angapradakshinam. They are willing to endure this hardship as proof of their devotion to Venkateswara. It is a way to surrender themselves and their problems to his care. It's similar to the arduous walk up the hill to reach the temple. Remember, some people even do the climb on their hands and knees? Also, the hours and hours of waiting and standing in queues just to get a glimpse of

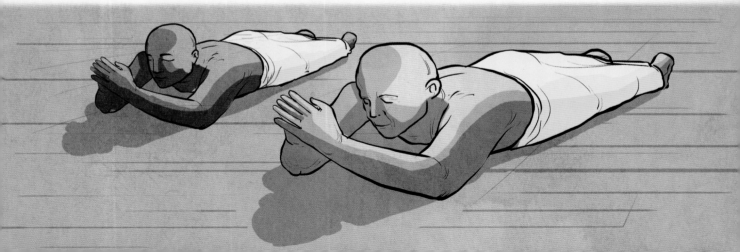

the deity is equally hard. And yet no one complains and people do all of this happily, as they believe that Venkateswara's blessings have the power to make their wishes come true. It is this faith that draws so many people here day after day, year after year.'

'But do their wishes really come true, Amma?' asked Shiv.

'That's a good question, Shiv,' said Amma. 'I believe they do. I believe that faith in one's God and the conviction that He is looking over us is what gives us the strength and will to work hard and make our wishes come true.'

Shiv and Veer looked thoughtful and fell silent.

The crowd surged forward into the room that led to the sanctum. Packed into the tight space, people rubbed shoulders with each other, not minding that their toes were being trodden on or that they were in such close proximity to strangers. In front of them was a set of gold-plated doors, bearing carvings of Vishnu in his various incarnations. These doors were also flanked, by two huge gilded statues—each with a conch, a disc and a mace in its hands.

'Look, it's Jaya and Vijaya again, whose statues we saw when we were entering Tirumala,' said Amma. 'The chief guards of Vishnu are doing their job protecting the entrance to his house. Do you see the closed golden doors between them?'

Shiv and Veer nodded excitedly.

'They are called Bangaru Vakili,' she continued, 'meaning "doors of gold".'

'Another door, Amma!' Veer pointed out. 'There are *so* many doors here!'

'Shh!' shushed Amma as a group of priests came forward and stood in two rows facing each other, forming a passage in front of the glimmering doors. They wore white dhotis with red, blue and green silk shawls draped over their shoulders and had microphones positioned in front of them. A hush fell over the crowd.

'Shiv, Veer, get ready for the famous Suprabhatam ceremony,' whispered Amma.

The priests started singing, their voices booming. The powerful rhythmic chanting of the Sanskrit hymns reverberated through the temple walls, drowning the gathered devotees in a tidal wave of harmony that filled every ear, heart and soul. '*Kausalya Supraja*

Rama! Purva Sandhya Pravartate . . .' they recited. Even though Shiv and Veer did not understand the words, they were spellbound by the music, their bodies gently swaying to the tune of the priests' chants.

Even after the priests had finished singing, the notes seemed to echo around them, and it took a minute or two for the gathering to recover control of their emotions, as if they were gradually released from the hold of a powerful hypnotic spell.

'Amma, what were they singing?' asked Shiv, still in awe.

'This is a hymn called "Suprabhatam", which means "auspicious dawn",' said Amma. 'It is the first song that is sung in the temple every morning. It was written in Sanskrit by a poet called Anantacharya more than 500 years ago.'

'That's such a long time ago! What does it mean?' asked Veer.

'Well, the song is a plea to Vishnu to wake up,' began Amma. 'It starts by saying, "O Rama, son of Kaushalya, dawn is approaching, wake up!" It cajoles him to get up by telling him how the sun is rising, the lotuses are blooming and the birds are chirping. It reminds him that he is the great protector and how, in his various avatars, he saved the world from evil. And that he needs to awaken and get to work again.'

'Amma, could you also sing to wake us up in the morning,' said Veer with a cheeky grin, 'instead of pulling the blankets off us?'

Amma giggled. 'Yes, my little Vishnu!' she said with a pat on his head.

'Why are the doors still closed?' asked Shiv. 'Is Venkateswara inside?'

'You see the figures of Vishnu's avatars?' asked Amma, pointing to the carvings on the doors.

'Yes,' came the reply in unison.

'The hymns were being sung to those incarnations,' said Amma. 'That's why the doors are closed. The other reason why the doors are shut is that Venkateswara is being given a ceremonial bath inside.'

'What do you mean?' asked Veer.

'Every morning, a small silver idol of Venkateswara is given a bath with milk and turmeric while "Suprabhatam" is being recited,' said Amma. 'Only after that can one see him—'

But before Amma could say more, the golden doors swung open! The crowd rushed forward like a winding snake, spilling into the final passage that led to the deity of Venkateswara. The moving serpent swallowed Amma, Shiv and Veer as they took their last few steps to see the lord of the hills.

The long, narrow corridor was illuminated by flickering oil lamps. As people walked in a line, their hands held high over their heads in a namaste, shifting shadows were cast on the walls. Hundreds of eyes strained to look ahead, desperate to catch their first glimpse of the deity. Amma held on tightly to the boys' hands as they inched ahead, following the queue, excited that their wait would soon be over.

And then they were in front of him. A lofty figure carved out of black granite looked down upon them with an all-knowing gaze full of kindness. His lips bloomed in an

eternal smile and his forehead was adorned by a mark of white camphor with a shining red tilak in the middle, streaked between half-opened eyes all the way to the tip of his nose. He was bedecked from head to toe in the most magnificent jewellery the boys had ever seen. A tall crown, made of gold and studded with diamonds, with a large emerald set in the centre, rested on his head. Crocodile-shaped earrings hung from his ears and a thick girdle of gold was strapped around his waist. He wore several necklaces, one with a pair of gold-encased tiger claws and another with the thousand names of Vishnu engraved on it. Armlets shaped like hooded cobras, golden bracelets, a pair of anklets and garlands strung from freshly plucked colourful flowers made up the rest of his attire. Two intricately carved golden plaques rested on either side of his chest, the image of Goddess Lakshmi seated on a lotus on the left and that of Goddess Padmavati on the right. There he stood in all his glory, the lord of the hills: Venkateswara.

Amma, Shiv and Veer were transfixed by the divine vision in front of them. For a few precious moments, they were oblivious to everything except for the deep connection that they felt with the deity. It was as if they were alone in the temple with Venkateswara, as their senses blocked out the sound and the smell of the crush pressing up against them.

But they were soon jolted out of their reverie by the temple attendants, who gently nudged them to move forward. Reluctantly, they started walking away, following the lines of devotees headed towards the sanctum's exit, even as their heads were turned to keep the deity in sight for as long as they could.

Once outside, they sat down on the floor facing the Garbha Griha. Some people were touching their foreheads to the walls of the sanctum while others were prostrating themselves on the ground with folded hands stretched out in front.

'That was so short! I wanted to stay longer, Amma,' Shiv complained, looking longingly at the golden doors leading to the sanctum.

'I did too,' said Amma, following his gaze. After a pause, she asked, 'So, what did you boys think of Venkateswara?'

'He is beautiful!' breathed Shiv, wide-eyed.

'He looked so real,' added Veer, and Shiv nodded in agreement.

'Yes, indeed, he did!' said Amma. 'I felt like he was blessing us.'

They were all quiet for some time as they relived the few seconds that they had spent looking at the glorious figure of Venkateswara.

'Oh, we found the treasure, Amma!' Veer gushed, breaking the silence. 'Venkateswara was wearing it!'

'No, Veer, the real treasure is Venkateswara himself, and not the jewels that he wears,' said Amma with a laugh.

'He does wear a lot of jewellery, doesn't he?' said Shiv.

'He sure does,' said Amma. 'His jewellery weighs more than the two of you put together! Do you know why he is wearing so many jewels, though? Because he is said to be dressed as a bridegroom.'

'Bridegroom? You mean he is getting married?' asked Shiv. 'I thought he was already married to Goddess Lakshmi.'

'Yes, as Vishnu he was married to Lakshmi, but as Venkateswara he married the princess Padmavati,' explained Amma.

'What? He has two wives?' inquired Veer.

'Well . . . yes and no, since Princess Padmavati was really an incarnation of Lakshmi,' said Amma. 'There is an interesting story behind it.'

'Tell us now! Tell us now!' chanted Shiv and Veer, tugging at Amma's dupatta.

'First, you tell me, did any of you see the engravings of Goddess Lakshmi and Goddess Padmavati on his chest?' asked Amma.

'Nope,' said Veer.

'Story! Story!' insisted Shiv.

'The story is told on that wall right over there, you two,' said Amma, pointing to a row of images carved on the stone wall opposite the Garbha Griha.

'So what do you see?' asked Amma once they'd walked over to inspect the bas-reliefs.

'Um . . . I see a cow and a calf,' said Veer confidently, looking at a sculpture. 'Is that from the story you told us?'

'Look!' yelled Shiv. 'There's Vishnu in the anthill. And there he is meeting Sri Varaha!'

'Well done! I'll tell you the rest of the story once we are outside,' said Amma as she guided them along the path circling the temple.

They had barely taken a few steps when they saw a crowd gathered around a large white cloth bag held up by two steel brackets that were attached to the walls on either side. Devotees were jostling to put notes and coins in it.

'Ah, so this is the famous *hundi*!' exclaimed Amma.

'Why are people putting money in it?' asked Veer.

'Many devotees gift money and precious jewels to Venkateswara,' said Amma. 'This is a bag to collect them.'

Amma reached into her purse, brought out some money and handed it to Shiv and Veer to put in the hundi. They made their way through the crowd and she lifted Shiv up so he could tip the notes in the bag. Veer got his turn next.

'Why did we give him money?' asked Shiv as they continued making their way out of the temple.

'It's to help Venkateswara repay a loan that he had taken from Kubera, the god of wealth, to pay for his wedding,' answered Amma.

'Huh?' asked Shiv. 'Why did Venkateswara need to borrow money? Didn't he have any?'

'You'll find out soon,' promised Amma. 'For now, can you guess how much money people give him every day?'

'One million rupees!' guessed Veer.

'Twenty-five to thirty million rupees!' announced Amma.

Shiv and Veer let out a loud gasp.

'Is he the richest god in the world?' asked Veer.

'Yes, indeed, he is!' said Amma. 'This is one of the richest temples in the world too. The money is used to maintain the temple and to run schools and hospitals.'

'Has he repaid his loan to Kubera by now?' asked Shiv.

'I would think so,' said Amma with a smile.

The three of them turned the corner and exited through the silver doors by which they had entered a short while ago. Outside, on their left, stood three tall copper statues. The figure of a handsome warrior-like man in green and red silk, wearing a crown, stood between the statues of two women dressed in elegant silk saris.

'Who are they, Amma?' asked Veer.

'This is a statue of the emperor Krishna Deva Raya, one of the greatest kings of the Vijayanagara Empire,' said Amma, indicating the figure in the middle. 'Remember the statue of the emperor we saw when we entered through the main door?'

'The one who was dressed in red?' asked Shiv.

'Yes, good memory!' said Amma. 'Krishna Deva Raya was his ancestor. He was a great warrior and an ardent devotee of Venkateswara. He used to come here whenever he could and made many generous donations to the temple. The statues of the two ladies are of his wives, Chinna Devi and Tirumala Devi.'

'He also had two wives like Venkateswara!' exclaimed Veer. Looking at the statues closely, he added, 'And both of them look exactly the same!'

Amma and Shiv started laughing.

'And now for the most fun part!' said Amma as they walked out of the main doors and turned left to find a row of counters set against the temple wall. 'Let's go get our prasad. It's laddus!'

'Laddu time!' cried out Shiv and Veer, hurrying behind Amma.

No sooner had Amma got a packet of laddus than a tug of war began between the boys.

'I got it first,' shouted Shiv, yanking at the packet.

'No, *I* got it first!' said Veer, trying to pull it away.

'Stop it!' admonished Amma as she snatched the packet from them. 'This is prasad and not some candy that you can fight over. There is a laddu each for the two of you in there, so there's no need to argue.'

Amma sat them down in the sprawling courtyard and handed them their laddus. The sheepish boys were quiet as they sank their teeth into the huge treats.

'Isn't it delicious?' asked Amma, softening and reaching over to wipe some crumbs from Veer's chin.

'This is the bestest laddu I've ever had!' declared Veer.

'Yummy!' said Shiv. 'Look, it has raisins!'

'And cashews too!' added Veer.

'I see that! Can you guess how many laddus are made here every day?' asked Amma.

Shiv and Veer shrugged their shoulders, their mouths full.

'Three hundred thousand, and it takes 300 cooks to prepare them.'

'Wow!' said Veer. 'Then why did I get only one?'

'And half of it seems to be on your face,' teased Shiv.

'Because one is enough for you, Veer,' said Amma. 'You are eating the most famous laddu in the world. The Tirupati laddu is so popular that it has its own patent.'

'What does that mean?' asked Shiv.

'It means that they have their own secret recipe for making them,' said Amma. 'No one else can make and sell laddus and call them Tirupati laddus.'

'Can we steal the recipe?' asked Veer, giggling.

'No, my little thief!' said Amma. 'Now for the story of Venkateswara's wedding that you've been waiting for.'

'Finally!' exclaimed Shiv.

'Remember the story of how Vishnu arrived in these hills in the form of a man,

Venkateswara, and how he was injured by the cowherd?' asked Amma. 'And how he then met Sri Varaha Swamy, who gave him a place to stay?'

'Yes, that was Vishnu as a boar,' replied Veer.

'Clever boy,' said Amma. 'Sri Varaha Swamy also asked one of his devotees, an elderly lady called Vakula Devi, to look after Venkateswara and tend to his wound. You both know the story of Krishna and how he too was an avatar of Vishnu, don't you? Vakula Devi was none other than Yashoda, Krishna's foster mother, who was reborn to be reunited with her son from her previous life. Vakula Devi lovingly took care of Venkateswara and his injury healed shortly. The two lived together in a small cottage in these hills.

'One day, Venkateswara was called upon to tame a wild elephant that was running amok in the forest. Pursuing the beast, he followed it into a garden, where a beautiful princess named Padmavati was walking with her friends. Venkateswara was struck by her beauty and grace, and he gave up the chase. They started a conversation and soon fell in love with each other.

'When he went home, Venkateswara confided in Vakula Devi. "Mother," he said, "I have fallen in love with Princess Padmavati and want to marry her. Will you take my wedding proposal to her father?"

'"Padmavati is the king's daughter, my child," said Vakula Devi, surprised by his request. "We have no money, no means and no fame. The king will never agree to this proposal. How will I convince him?"

'"I am sure you will find a way, Mother," said Venkateswara with a persuasive smile.

'Encouraged by his confidence, Vakula Devi agreed to take her son's proposal to the king and immediately left for the city. Meanwhile, Venkateswara came up with a clever plan to help her in this difficult task. He disguised himself as a woman and, pretending to be a fortune teller, also set off for the palace.'

'He dressed like a girl!' chimed in Veer, giggling.

Smiling, Amma continued with the story. 'He reached the city before his mother and announced himself as a renowned astrologer. He arranged for an audience with Padmavati's mother, the queen.

'"Tell me, fortune teller," said the queen upon meeting him, "what does the future hold for my daughter?"

'"Your daughter is not only blessed with beauty, but with luck as well," pronounced the fake fortune teller rather grandly. "She is destined to marry none other than Lord Vishnu himself. An elderly lady will soon arrive with a marriage proposal, which you must not refuse."

'With these words, the fortune teller departed, leaving the queen mystified. Soon thereafter, Vakula Devi reached the palace and asked the king for Padmavati's hand in marriage for her son, whom she described as a common forest dweller. Before the king

could react to this strange request from the elderly lady, the queen quickly told him about the fortune teller's prediction. "We must accept this proposal," she said, "for I am convinced it is from Lord Vishnu himself."

'The king immediately consented. The royal sages were consulted for an auspicious time, and the wedding date was set. Venkateswara was delighted when he heard the news, but he was also worried. How was he to pay for the lavish wedding ceremony and how was he to acquire the wealth needed to provide his bride with the comforts that she was used to?'

'That's when he went to Kubera and asked him for a loan!' piped up Shiv.

'You've got it! Aren't the stories falling into place now?' said Amma. 'Kubera, the god of wealth, agreed to give Venkateswara the money he needed. Preparations for the ceremony began and invitations were sent out to everyone on earth as well as in the heavens. Gods and goddesses descended to earth and joined the glorious wedding procession that had Venkateswara at its head, atop his divine mount, the eagle Garuda. Venkateswara and Padmavati were married in a grand ceremony, the likes of which had never been witnessed before.

'They started living together happily amid the beauty of the gardens, mountains and waterfalls of the Tirumala hills.

'Then came a time when people's belief in gods and goddesses weakened,' Amma continued. 'This saddened Vishnu, who felt that he was no longer valued on earth. So he decided to return to the heavens, leaving behind a stone statue of his form for his true devotees.'

'That's the statue we saw?' asked Shiv and Veer together.

'Yes,' said Amma. 'For many years, the statue stood in the middle of a simple open pavilion. Years later, a temple was built to house the statue. Over the next hundreds of years, the temple became very popular because kings of powerful dynasties—like the Pallavas, the Cholas and those of the Vijayanagara Empire—who ruled over southern India worshipped at the temple and donated many expensive gifts. Remember, we saw statues of a couple of these kings inside?'

'Uh-huh,' said Veer.

'There is another story about how Venkateswara became a stone statue, a funny one that I like more,' said Amma with a wink.

'Tell us! Tell us!' said Shiv and Veer in unison.

'You remember that Lakshmi had fought with Vishnu and, leaving him, had come down to earth?' reminded Amma.

Shiv and Veer nodded even as Amma continued. 'Lakshmi was in deep meditation by River Godavari when the clever sage Narada decided to pay her a visit.

'"Narada, how is Lord Vishnu?" asked Lakshmi upon meeting the sage.

'"He is very well indeed!" said Narada mischievously. "And quite happy with his new wife."

'"*What?*" said Lakshmi, shocked. "He has taken another wife?"

'The news was too much for her to bear. Seething with rage, she made her way to

Venkatadri Hill, where she found Venkateswara and Padmavati strolling around. She immediately recognized that Venkateswara was none other than Vishnu, of course. Her anger knew no bounds.

'"How could you do this to me?" she demanded, confronting Venkateswara.

'But Venkateswara was speechless. Then she turned to Padmavati.

'"What are you doing with my husband?" shouted Lakshmi. "Don't you know that he is married to me?"

'"What do you mean?" said Padmavati. "He married me!"

'"In that case," said Lakshmi, "why don't we ask *him* who his wife is?"

'Meanwhile, Venkateswara had quietly taken a few steps back.

'"Can you please . . ." Lakshmi began, turning to look at Venkateswara. She was stunned. For in place of her husband now stood a lifeless statue!'

'What!' blurted Shiv.

'How did that happen?' asked Veer.

'Well, Vishnu did not want to face both his wives and be part of their fight,' said Amma. 'So he turned to stone! I suppose it's not just your father who is scared of me,' she added with a mischievous grin. 'It seems that even gods are scared of their wives!'

'I'm going to tell Daddy that you said he's scared of you!' teased Shiv.

Veer started giggling.

'Telltale!' said Amma before continuing with the story. 'Lord Brahma and Lord Shiva then appeared before the confused queens and explained the purpose behind Lord Vishnu's incarnation as Venkateswara—to protect the people on earth. They also told Lakshmi that Princess Padmavati was none other than an incarnation of Lakshmi herself, born as a mortal to marry her lord again on earth. When gods and goddesses come to earth in different avatars, they can coexist and sometimes may not recognize their other forms immediately.'

'Like Varaha Swamy and Venkateswara!' chirped Veer.

'Exactly!' said Amma. 'That is why Lakshmi had to be reminded that Princess Padmavati was none other than she herself.'

'Then what happened?' asked Shiv. 'Did Lakshmi calm down?'

'Lakshmi was finally appeased,' said Amma. 'She returned to join Venkateswara on the hill and made her home in his heart. And that is how Vishnu gets the name Srinivasa, "the place where Lakshmi or Sri resides". Vishnu even told Lakshmi about his debt to Kubera. To help him repay the loan, she agreed to enrich the devotees who offer him money and gold, and so it is believed that people who give gifts to Venkateswara earn the blessings of Lakshmi, the goddess of wealth, too.'

'So when we put money in the hundi to help Venkateswara pay off his debt to Kubera, Lakshmi blessed us? Cool!' said Shiv.

'Interesting, isn't it? Also, Lakshmi and Padmavati said that they wished to be with Vishnu forever and also turned into stone idols. Lakshmi stayed with him on the left side of his chest while Padmavati rested on the right.'

'So that's why there are images of Lakshmi and Padmavati on Venkateswara's chest,' said Veer.

'Yes, smarty-pants,' said Amma, ruffling Veer's hair. 'So that is the story of Venkateswara and how he became the lord of these hills. And that,' she added, letting out a big breath, 'is also the last story the two of you will get for a while. C'mon, it's time for us to head back.' She stood up and beckoned for Shiv and Veer to follow.

It was nearing dawn and the darkness of the night sky was beginning to make way for the light of the rising sun. The two boys took in the magnificent surroundings one last time as they got up reluctantly, stretched and walked across the courtyard towards the car park with Amma.

'There is one final thing that I may have forgotten to tell you,' said Amma, slowing down to look at them.

'What?' the boys asked together, hoping that another long story was on its way.

'I saved an extra laddu for you guys . . . but if you don't want it, I'm happy to eat it,' said Amma as she sneakily brought out a packet from her bag.

'Ladduuuuu!' shrieked Shiv and Veer at once, chasing Amma across the courtyard.

DASHAVATAR

1 MATSYA

3 VARAHA

2 KURMA

4 NARASIMHA

5 VAMANA

THE TEN AVATARS OF VISHNU

6 PARASHURAMA

8 BALARAMA

7 RAMA

9 KRISHNA

10 KALKI

ACKNOWLEDGEMENTS

Writing this book has been quite the journey, and I have been lucky in my fellow travellers, who have unstintingly supported me every step of the way.

My husband, Anurag—my best friend, my soulmate—who supports me with an unwavering love and generosity that I am grateful for every day and without whom this book would have been a jumble of notes in my writing pad. Thank you for walking with me, for understanding my madness and never doubting me.

My little men, Shiv and Veer, who bring me so much joy. I hope that this book can be an answer to some of your whys, hows and whens.

Fabulous friends Sangeeta Bajaj and Alka Sanghi, who made it possible for me to see Venkateswara in all his glory. I am forever indebted to you.

Fellow journey-women, Sapna and Schauna Malhotra, for making this trip so memorable.

Sohini Mitra, my fantastic editor at Penguin, for coming up with the idea for the series and convincing me to write it. I am so happy that you didn't give up on me.

The team at Penguin India, who worked tirelessly on this book.

Page Richards, the wonderful head of the MFA programme at Hong Kong University, and my advisers, Brittani Sonnenburg and Michelle Sterling, for guiding me through this process and helping the story find its shape and place.

My friends from the MFA programme—Anthony, Janet, Judy, Manisha, Rinkoo and Sharon—for your patience and insights while enduring my numerous drafts.

To the wonderful members of the Society of Children's Book Writers and Illustrators—Elizabeth, Janet, John, Kris, Larry, Mio, Rachel, Ritu, Skye and Virginie—for being such enthusiastic readers of my drafts and for encouraging me to find my voice.

A HISTORICAL TIMELINE OF
SRI VENKATESWARA SWAMY TEMPLE

✦ **2nd century** The earliest mentions of the Tirumala hills are traced to Tamil poets Tholkappiar, who refers to them as the northern boundary of the Tamil world, and Mamulanar, who refers to them as the Vendagam hills, which had attained fame for its festive celebrations during the year.

✦ **2nd–3rd centuries** The first reference to a deity appears in the Silappadikaaram, a Tamil epic thought to be written by Jain prince Ilango Adigal, which alludes to the shrine in Vendagam as being one devoted to Vishnu. The author says, 'Lord Vishnu of the lotus eyes is seen in a standing posture on the top of Vendagam Hill, which is full of waterfalls and where the rays of the sun and the moon shine on the image.' This indicates that the figure was out in the open and that no temple had been built yet. During this time, the Vaishnava saints of Tamil Nadu, called *alvar*s, venerate Tirumala and compose and sing songs in praise of the lord of Vendagam.

✦ **5th–6th centuries** The Puranas ascribe the construction of the temple to a king named Thondaiman, then ruler of Narayanavanam, who discovers the image of the god 'standing under a tree, with the lower part of the body hidden in an anthill' while climbing the hill with a local hunter. He is said to have commissioned the building of the initial temple compound and perhaps even the original temple complex.

✦ **9th–10th centuries** The Pallava dynasty of Kanchipuram and the Chola dynasty of Thanjavur are devoted to Lord Venkateswara and the royalty visits the temple regularly.

✦ **11th century** Ramanuja, a great Hindu philosopher and one of the biggest proponents of Vaishnavism (the branch of Hinduism that considers Vishnu to be the supreme being), establishes the temple as a Vaishnava site and lays down many of the methods and details of worship.

✦ **14th–15th centuries** The temple gains most of its current wealth and prominence under the rulers of the Vijayanagara Empire, with its donations of gold and diamonds. One of the main patrons of the temple, Emperor Krishna Deva Raya, enables the dome Ananda Nilayam to be gilded.

* **15th century** Tallapaka Annamacharya, a Hindu bard, composes around 32,000 *sankirtana*s or devotional songs in praise of Venkateswara. It is said that not a single day passed in his life without him composing at least one song dedicated to Venkateswara.

* **16th–17th centuries** Maratha rulers and the kings of Mysore foster the growth of the temple.

* **17th–18th centuries** The Tirumala region is ruled by Muslim dynasties—the sultans of Golconda and the nawabs of the Carnatic—who extract tributes and taxes from the temples.

* **1801** The management and revenue of the temple pass to the East India Company.

* **1843–1933** The administration of the temple is entrusted by the East India Company to Sri Deva Dossiji of the Hathiramji Mutt in Tirumala. It remains in the charge of the mahants of the organization for ninety years.

* **1933** A trust called Tirumala Tirupati Devasthanams (TTD) is set up to oversee the running of the temple. Since then, the temple has been successfully managed by the TTD.

DAILY PRAYERS

The daily prayers, or *seva*s, that are performed for the main deity of Lord Venkateswara commence with Suprabhatam, followed by Thomala Seva and Archana Seva, and conclude with Ekantha Seva.

* **Suprabhatam** is the first seva of the day, performed at 2.30 a.m. at Sayana Mandapam inside the sanctum sanctorum, to rouse the lord from his celestial sleep with the rhythmic chanting of Vedic hymns. The Suprabhatam comprises Sanskrit *shloka*s sung in praise of the lord.
* **Thomala Seva** is the decoration of the statue of Venkateswara with colourful flower-and-tulsi garlands after awakening him. 'Thomala' comes from the Tamil expression *thodutha malai*, meaning 'a garland of strung flowers'.
* **Sahasranama Archana** is the recitation of the 1008 names of Lord Venkateswara.
* **Ekantha Seva** is the last ritual of the day, for which Bhoga Srinivasa (a silver replica of the main deity) is seated in a golden cot inside Sayana Mandapam. A velvet bed is spread on the swing, and milk and fruit are offered to him to the accompaniment of music, before the lord is left alone for a good night's rest. After this seva is performed, the temple is closed for the night.

Some sevas are performed after hours for the processional deity of Lord Venkateswara, who is known as Malayappa Swamy. **Sahasra Deepalankara Seva** is one of them—the lighting of a thousand oil lamps outside the temple premises.

GLOSSARY

Balaji: Another name for Venkateswara. Derived from the Sanskrit word *bala*, which means 'baby' or 'youthful'

Brahma: The god of all creation in Hinduism. The holy trinity of gods includes: Brahma, the creator; Vishnu, the protector; and Shiva, the destroyer.

Garbha Griha: The innermost sanctum of a temple, where the idol of the primary deity resides. The term literally means 'womb chamber'.

Govardhan: A hill located near the town of Vrindavan, the name means 'the mountain that nourishes cows'. The word *go* translates to 'cow' and *vardhana*, to 'nourishment'.

Govinda: Another name for Krishna—who is an avatar of Vishnu—it means 'cowherd'.

Hanuman: A loyal devotee of Rama and one of the key figures in the epic Ramayana. He is the son of Anjana, a celestial nymph, and Kesari, a monkey king. The wind god, Vayu, is said to have had a hand in his birth.

Kaliya: The poisonous snake on whose head Krishna danced, in a river in Vrindavan, thus overpowering him

Krishna: The ninth avatar of Vishnu and a central character in the epic Mahabharata. Also the narrator of the Bhagavad Gita (The Song of God), one of Hinduism's most popular scriptures based on the dialogue between Krishna and Arjuna on the battlefield of Kurukshetra

Namaste: A respectful greeting in the Hindu tradition

Rama: The seventh avatar of Vishnu and the central figure of the Ramayana, he is considered to be one of the most important avatars of the protector god, along with Krishna.

Shiva: The god among the holy trinity who is believed to play the role of the 'destroyer' or 'transformer' to maintain balance in the universe

Telugu: The primary language in the states of Andhra Pradesh and Telangana

Tirumala: The small town situated near Tirupati in Chittoor district of Andhra Pradesh. The word *tiru* means 'sacred' and *mala* means 'mountain'. Hence Tirumala means 'holy mountain'.

Tirupati: Literally 'the husband of Lakshmi'. The word 'tiru' also translates to Lakshmi, and the word *pati* means 'husband'.

Vijayanagara Empire: The empire was founded in 1336 by brothers Harihara I and Bukka Raya I, and their rule lasted for about three centuries.

SELECTED BIBLIOGRAPHY

I am grateful to the following authors for their detailed works, which guided me in writing this book.

* Aiyangar, S. Krishnasvami. *A History of Tirupati*. UK: Lightning Source, n.d. Reprinted by Nabu Public Domain Reprints.

* Annamayya. *God on the Hill: Temple Poems from Tirupati*. Translated by Velcheru Narayana Rao and David Shulman. New York: Oxford University Press, 2005.

* Charya, T.K.T. Viraraghava. *History of Tirupati* (Volumes 1–3). Tirupati: Tirumala Tirupati Devasthanams, 2009.

* Neelima, Kota. *Tirupati: A Guide to Life*. Noida: Random House India, 2012.

* Krishna, Nanditha. *Balaji-Venkateshwara: Lord of Tirumala-Tirupati*. Mumbai: Vakils, Feffer & Simons, 2000.

* ———. *The Book of Vishnu*. New Delhi: Penguin Books India, 2001.

* Pattanaik, Devdutt. *7 Secrets of Vishnu*. Chennai: Westland, 2011.

* Ramesan, N. *The Tirumala Temple*. Tirupati: Tirumala Tirupati Devasthanams, 2009.

Other sources, including websites,* documentaries and articles, referred to:

* *Indiatimes*. 'The Tirupati Laddu Turns 300.' 6 August 2015. https://www.indiatimes.com/news/india/the-tirupati-laddu-turns-300_-243893.html.

* Kondapalli, Rajendra Srivathsa. *Inside Tirumala Tirupati*. A National Geographic exclusive. Pulse Media Production, 27 March 2017.

---

* Content and URL may have changed since last accessed.

✤   Nair, Roshni. 'Shear Devotion: The Barbers of Tirupati.' *DNA India*. Last modified 5 July 2015. http://www.dnaindia.com/lifestyle/report-shear-devotion-the-barbers-of-tirupati-2101788.

✤   *The Hindu*. 'Tirumala Temple Hundi Still Open for Rs 1000, Rs 500 Notes.' 12 November 2016, Chennai edition. http://www.thehindu.com/news/national/andhra-pradesh/Tirumala-temple-hundi-still-open-for-Rs.-1000-Rs.-500-notes/article16443055.ece.

✤   Tirumala Tirupati Devasthanams. Last accessed 28 October 2017. http://www.tirumala.org/.

✤   Trip Advisor India. 'Tirupati' (reviews). Last accessed 28 October 2017. https://en.tripadvisor.com.hk/ShowUserReviews-g297587-d1220147-r187366818-Tirumala_Temple-Tirupati_Chittoor_District_Andhra_Pradesh.html.

READ MORE IN THE SERIES
Amma, Take Me to the Golden Temple

COME, EXPLORE THE PLACES WHERE WE WORSHIP!

Join Amma and her children as they travel to the famous Golden Temple in Amritsar, the holiest seat of Sikhism.

Take a tour through the wonderful sights and sounds of Harmandir Sahib. Hear inspiring stories about the Sikh gurus. Discover the rich heritage of the Darshani Deori and the Akal Takht. Take a sip from the sacred waters at Har ki Pauri and savour the hearty langar offered by the world's biggest kitchen. Learn Guru Nanak's eternal message of equality, love and service. Listen to Amma with your eyes and ears wide open, for this whirlwind of a journey promises to leave you mesmerized!

Told through interesting stories with captivating illustrations, this new series introduces readers to the history of different faiths and their associated monuments that draw thousands and thousands of enthusiastic visitors every day.

'Contains a wealth of detail . . . The lively text is complemented by excellent illustrations' *The Hindu*

'A treat of a read. Mathur has a fine eye for detail and strikes a perfect balance between history, folklore, information and anecdote. [The] illustrations . . . make the narrative sparkle and [make] us eager for the rest of the series' *Indian Express*

'Beautifully weaves the intricate history and different aspects of Sikhism in the narration' *Asian Age*